EASY HOME
IMPROVEMENTS

your closets and storage

EASY HOME IMPROVEMENTS

your closets and storage

STEWART WALTON

LEBHAR-FRIEDMAN BOOKS

New York • Chicago • Los Angeles • London • Paris • Tokyo

Lebhar-Friedman Books
425 Park Avenue
New York, NY 10022

First U.S. edition published 2000 by Lebhar-Friedman Books
Copyright © 2000 Marshall Editions Ltd., London U. K.

Published by Lebhar-Friedman Books
Lebhar-Friedman Books is a company of Lebhar-Friedman, Inc.

Originated in Singapore by Pica.
Printed and bound in China by Excel Printing.

Library of Congress Cataloging-In-Publication Data:
On file at Library of Congress
ISBN: 0-86730-790-0

Project Editor Ian Kearey

Designed by Paul Griffin

Photographer Alistair Hughes

Managing Editor Antonia Cunningham

Managing Art Editor Patrick Carpenter

Editorial Director Ellen Dupont

Art Director Dave Goodman

Editorial Coordinator Ros Highstead

Production Amanda Mackie

Indexer Jill Dormon

Front cover photography: **J. Pilkington/ The Interior Archive**
Back cover: **Alistair Hughes**

Visit our Web site at lfbooks.com

Volume Discounts
This book makes a great gift and incentive. Call (212) 756-5240 for
information on volume discounts.

Note

contents

introduction

For most of us, finding places to keep things neatly is a perennial problem—shoes, toys, books, and magazines, to name a few objects, have a habit of spreading themselves everywhere. There are two practical ways to solve this: the first, throwing everything but the very bare essentials out and living a spartan, minimalist, and rugged life, is achieved (or even desired) only by a small minority; the rest of us have to follow the second line, that of least resistance, and purchase or make storage solutions. A brief look in all but the most expensive stores will show that attractive designs don't always mean the best quality of materials or construction, so take pride in your work and make your own!

In this book, I designed the projects to be accessible to as wide a range of people as possible. In the introduction to each set of step-by-step photographs and text, the project is given a skill rating of Beginner, Intermediate, or Advanced. Of course in the wardrobe with loose fabric cover, to give just one example, someone with experience in woodworking, for whom cutting joints poses no problem, may find using a sewing machine a tough proposition, and the reverse will be true for a practiced tailor or seamstress.

The important thing is to look at all the stages of each project before you tackle it and, above all, take your time— the times given in the introductory section for the projects assume you have all the materials and tools on hand and can

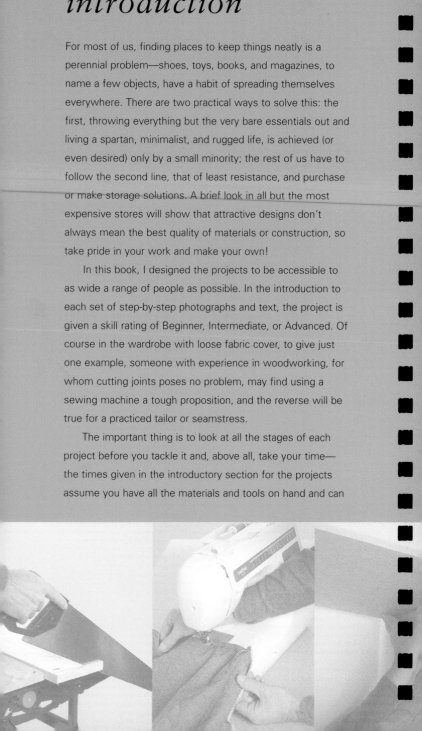

work uninterruptedly until you have finished. The additional work needed to finish a project—treating wood, applying protection, painting, and varnishing—are not included in the times, nor are drying times for glue, wood putty, and finishes.

Note that the dimensions given in the Materials lists are for the finished size of each component as made for this book; you can adapt the projects to fit your own requirements, particularly those made to fit a particular alcove or similar space. If you are planning to change the size radically, you may have to reconsider the width and depth you use for each component, both for strength and proportions.

When it comes to tools, the golden rule is that you get what you pay for. Inexpensive tools may seem a bargain, but their drawbacks can range from measuring inaccurately to falling apart while working—and for power tools, this can lead to injury or worse. Make a careful check on secondhand tools, and inspect the wiring in electrical tools.

Don't let these dire warnings put you off. If you follow the manufacturer's instructions, and wear protective clothing where necessary, you should not have a problem. Good tools do cost, so build up your tool kit as and when you can; and to save spending money on equipment that may only be used once or twice, most rental stores hire out large and small power tools by the day or weekend.

I hope you get enjoyment and a sense of having achieved something worthwhile out of these projects.

Stewart Walton

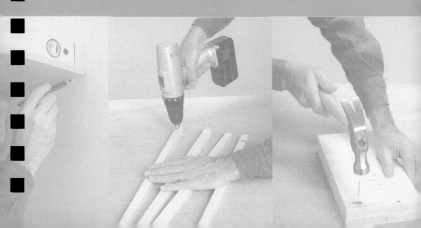

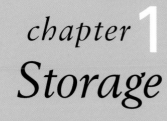

chapter 1
Storage

making a
toy box

Children's toys seem to have a mind of their own, and spend much of their time not being where they should be—so a sturdy storage box is pretty essential. Even if you don't have children, the box can be used for keeping a variety of things in, and the casters mean you can take it from room to room as it is needed. You can paint cheerful, contrasting colors to brighten up or match a room, or think about more adventurous decorative techniques, such as stencilling or freehand painting.

Materials (all lumber is MDF unless otherwise stated)

2 pieces 18 x ¾ x 12⅞ in. • 1 piece 20 x ¾ x 18 in. • 1 piece 20 x ¾ x 15 in. • 1 piece 20 x ¾ x 10½ in. • 1 piece 20 x ¾ x 11½ in. • 1 piece softwood 20 x ⅝ x 1¼ in. • 2 pieces softwood 10½ x ⅝ x 1¼ in. • 1½-in. no. 6 screws • 1-in. no. 6 screws • 4 casters, 2 in. top to bottom

Tools

Jigsaw or coping saw • Crosscut saw • Combination square • Straightedge • Power or bench plane • Screwdriver • Drill with 1½ in., 1 in., and countersink bits • Abrasive paper and cork or foam block • PVA (white) glue • Wood putty

Skill level

Beginner/Intermediate

Time

2–3 hours

1 Cut the two sides to 18 x 12⅞ in. from ¾ in. MDF, and check the corners for square. Position a 6-in. baking tin or plate so that it's touching the two front edges of the sides, and draw a curve around the top of the plate with a pencil.

2 Shade in the waste MDF and cut around the curve—a power jigsaw makes this task easy, otherwise you can use a coping saw. Check that both sides are identical, and sand to adjust if required.

Helpful hints

MDF produces a lot of possibly harmful dust when sawed, drilled, or sanded. Wear a dust mask when working it, and use dust extractors if fitted to your power tools.

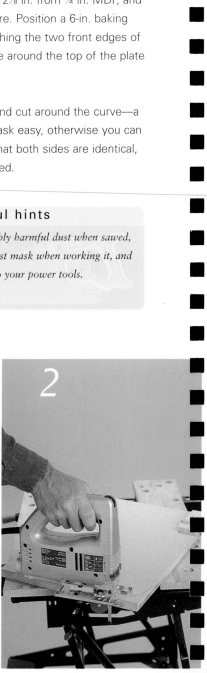

3 Cut the box lid to 20 x 11½ in. from ¾ in. MDF. Check that the corners are square, then use the plate or tin to trace the curves for the openings at each end—the holes should start 3½ in. from the front edge and 3 in. from the back. Shade the waste and cut with a power jigsaw or coping saw.

4 Clamp the lid in your workbench or vise, and plane and sand down the sides to produce a rounded finish. Cut the back to 20 x 18 in. and the front to 20 x 15 in. from ¾ in. MDF.

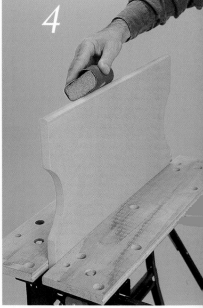

5 Mark out positional guides on the side panels for the positions of the back, front, and base, using the actual pieces to mark out lines for an exact fit. The bottom of the base should finish 1¼ in. above the bottom of the sides, back, and front, to allow for the casters.

6 Cut the two base battens to 10½ in. from ⅝ x 1¼ in. softwood. Mark, drill, and countersink three pilot holes in each batten, then place each in turn against one side with its top edge meeting the base line. Mark through the pilot holes with a bradawl, then screw in place using 1½-in. no. 6 screws.

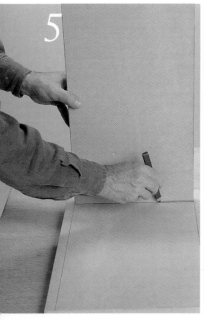

7 Lay the back and one side butted up together, with their bottom edges meeting exactly. Using a square and straightedge, draw a horizontal line from the top of the front position on the sides along the back. This is the lower edge of the lid batten. Cut the batten to 20 in. from ⅝ x 1¼ in. softwood, drill and countersink three pilot holes, apply glue, and insert and drive in 1-in. no. 6 screws.

8 Lay the back flat and hold one side vertically in position, checking for square. Mark and drill three equidistant screw holes along the side inside the marked lines. Drill pilot holes through the sides into the back and countersink them, then apply glue and drive in 1½-in. no. 6 screws.

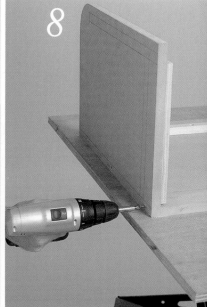

9 Position the base so it sits in place on top of the base battens. As for the sides, drill and countersink two equidistant pilot holes through the sides inside the marked lines, then apply glue and drive in 1½-in. no. 6 screws.

10 Hold the front position the same way as in steps 8 and 9. Drill and countersink two pilot holes through the sides and three along the front into the base, then apply glue and drive in 1½-in. no. 6 screws.

11 Turn the box upside down and place each caster in position—near the corners but far away from the sides, front, and back to ensure that the wheels run freely. Mark the screw positions through the holes in the casters with a pencil, then bradawl the holes and drive in the screws firmly.

12 Fill all the screw holes with wood putty and a putty knife, allow to dry, and sand smooth. Give the whole box and lid a final light sanding, wipe off, then paint using alkyd or semi-matte water-base paint—you don't need to use primer on MDF.

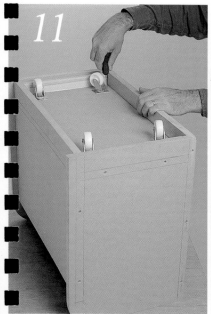

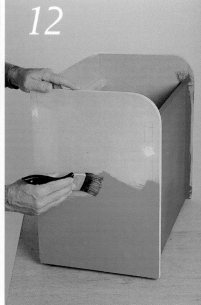

making a hall settle

Settles with hinge-opening or removable seats or lids and storage room inside have been popular pieces of furniture for centuries. The earliest known examples were made of dark, long-lasting hardwood; resin-bonded MDF, as used in this project, is claimed to have the same stability. This settle uses only butt joints and is glued and screwed together. If you have a large hall or wall space, consider extending the width, but keep the simple symmetry of this version.

Materials (all lumber is MDF unless otherwise stated)

1 piece 30 x ¾ x 28 in. • 2 pieces 19 x ¾ x 10½ in. • 1 piece 29½ x ¾ x 20 in. • 1 piece 31½ x ¾ x 9 in. • 1 piece 31½ x ¾ x 3 in. • 1 piece 31 x ¾ x 3½ in. • 1 piece 12 x ¾ x 3½ in. • 1 piece 28 x ¾ x 9¾ in. • 1 piece softwood 28 x ¾ x 1½ in. • 1½-in. no. 6 screws • 2 brass flush hinges 2 in. long with brass screws

Tools

Crosscut saw or jigsaw • Combination square • Miter saw • Straightedge • Bradawl • Pencil • Drill with pilot hole and countersink bits • Screwdriver • Abrasive paper and sanding block • Carpenter's level • PVA (white) glue • Wood putty • Filling knife

Skill level

Intermediate

Time

3–4 hours

1 Cut the back to 30 in. height and 28 in. width. Mark the top edge, then measure 11 in. from the top on each side and draw a line across the width. Mark 2 in. along the top from the edges and along the drawn line, then join the marks with a vertical line. Shade in the waste and mark a diagonal line between marks made 1 in. along the top and the vertical line.

2 Use a crosscut saw or jigsaw to cut out the waste MDF on each side, then cut along the diagonal lines to create bevels at the top. Sand the cut edges smooth with abrasive paper wrapped around a sanding block.

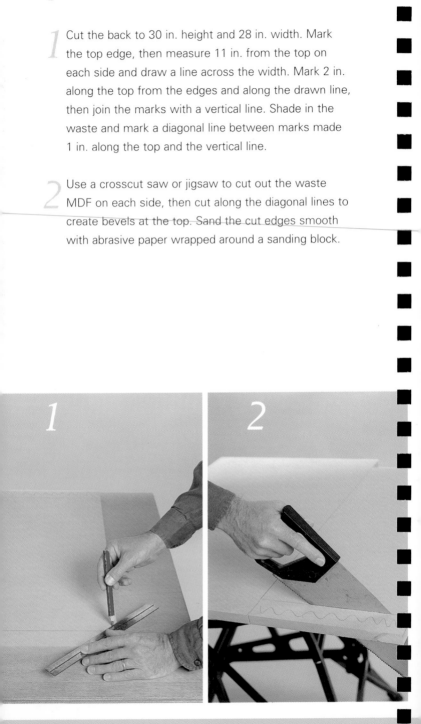

3 Cut a ¾ x 1½ in. piece of softwood to 28 in. and sand the ends. Drill and countersink three equidistant pilot holes through the batten and position it with its upper edge meeting the line across the back. Mark through the holes with a bradawl, apply glue, and drive in 1½-in. no. 6 screws.

4 Cut the two sides to 19 x 10½ in. Draw a line ¾ in. inside each back and base edge, and within this line mark, drill, and countersink three pilot holes for the back and two for the base.

5 Position one side to the back, with the top of the side level with the top of the batten and the rear edge of the back exactly meeting the edge of the side. Drill through the pilot holes into the side edge of the back, apply glue, then drive in 1½-in. no. 6 screws, making sure the corner is square. Repeat for the other side.

6 Cut the base to 28 x 9¾ in. Position it between the edge and drawn lines on the sides and drill pilot holes into the edges through the holes in the sides. Apply glue and drive in screws. Cut the front to 29½ x 20 in. and draw a line ¾ in. inside the side edges. Drill and countersink three pilot holes, then apply glue and screw to the sides as before.

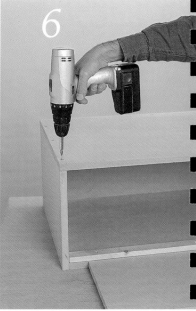

7 The movable lid and seat back are cut in one piece
initially. Measure and mark a piece of MDF to
31½ x 12 in., and cut it using a jigsaw or crosscut saw.

8 Lay the carcass on its back and position the lid/seat-
back piece butting up to the sides and front; the MDF
overhang at each side should be 1 in. Mark where this
piece meets the cut-out on the back and use a square
to draw a line across it. Measure ¾ in. along these
lines, join them, and cut out the waste to fit the back.

9 Position the carcass upright and fit the lid/seat-back piece in its place, butting up to the back firmly. Measure 3 in. along the sides of the lid/seat-back from the back and use a straightedge to draw a line across the piece. Cut the piece with a jigsaw or fine-tooth crosscut saw, then smooth the cut edges.

10 Use a square to draw two lines across the shallow piece (the seat-back) at the start of the cut-outs. Close the flush hinges and place them with their center on these marks, then butt up the lid with its sides meeting the seat-back sides exactly. Draw lines to meet the hinge ends across both pieces with a square.

11 Continue the lines onto the meeting edges of the seat-back and lid. Hold the seat-back on its rear edge, position the large part of the hinges to the lines, and mark and drill guide holes for the hinge screws. Drive in the screws, then hold the lid and seat pieces together and mark and drill guide holes in the lid and screw the hinges in place.

12 For the plinth side, cut one end of a length of ¾ x 3½ in. square, hold it against the rear of one side, and mark the front edge of the carcass. Set a miter saw to 45 degrees and cut a miter with the mark at the inner edge; the total length is 12 in. Repeat for the other side.

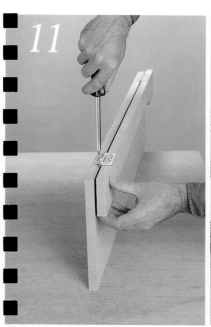

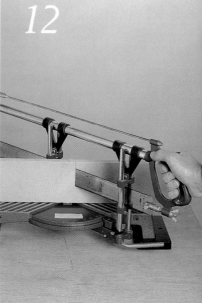

13 Clamp each plinth side in the workbench and use
medium-grade abrasive paper wrapped around a
sanding block to sand a bevel on the top front edge.
How big you make he bevel is a matter of personal
taste—here, it was about 45 degrees. If you wish,
draw lines on the top edge and front as guides.

14 Measure and miter the plinth front to 31 in., with the
miter facing in from the outer edge. Bevel the top as
in step 13. Position the plinth pieces with a 1-in.
overhang at the bottom of the sides and front, drill
and countersink three pilot holes for the front and two
for the sides, apply glue, and screw the plinth pieces
in place.

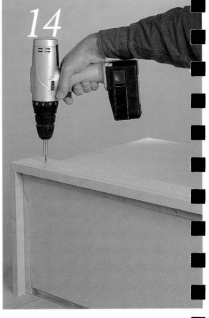

15 Stand the settle upright and position the lid/seat-back assembly against the back. Mark, drill, and countersink pilot holes through the seat-back to fix it to the back and sides. Make guide holes through the pilot holes, then apply glue and drive in screws.

16 Use a filling knife to push wood putty into the screw holes, leaving it protruding above the surface. Allow to dry completely and sand smooth. Dust off the settle and cover it with matte or gloss household paint.

Helpful hints

You can sand a small bevel on the top front and side edges of the opening lid, but make sure this is the same depth along the whole front and sides.

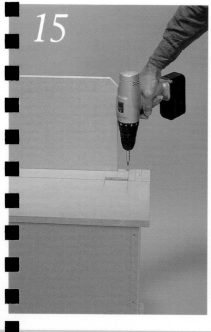

making a **bookcase**

This bookcase is designed to be constructed with the minimum of fuss—none of the screws used is driven in through the front or sides, thus cutting down the time needed for preparation before painting. The shelves are part of the carcass and don't just rest on the supports; where you position them will depend on the size of books (or photographs, ornaments, and so on) you intend to keep in the bookcase.

Materials (all lumber is MDF unless otherwise stated)

2 pieces 54 x ¾ x 12 in. • 4 pieces 16 x ¾ x 9 in. •
1 piece 54 x ¾ x 16 in. • 8 pieces softwood 9 x 1 x 1 in. •
4 pieces softwood 16 x ½ x 2½ in. • 1½ in.-no. 6 screws

Tools

Crosscut saw or jigsaw • Combination square • Straightedge •
Bradawl • Pencil • Drill with pilot hole and countersink bits •
Screwdriver • Medium-grade abrasive paper and sanding
block • Masking tape • PVA (white) glue

Skill level

Intermediate

Time

3–4 hours

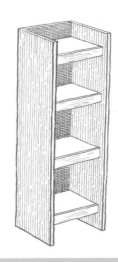

1 Measure and cut the four shelves to 16 x 9 in. from
¾ in. MDF. In this project the shelves are an integral
part of the carcass, so it is essential they are cut
square. To help you cut accurately, clamp a straight
piece of thick lumber to the cutting line to guide your
crosscut saw.

2 Check the shelves with a square after cutting, and
make sure all four pieces are identical. Make any
adjustments, then butt a strip of ½ x 2 in. softwood
up to the front edge of each shelf and mark the shelf
length exactly.

Helpful hints

*You can cut or sand a slight bevel on the front edges of the
shelf supports; measure 1 in. back from the front edge along
the lower side, draw diagonal lines to this on the sides, and
cut the bevel.*

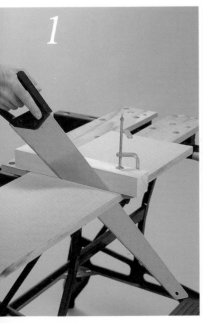

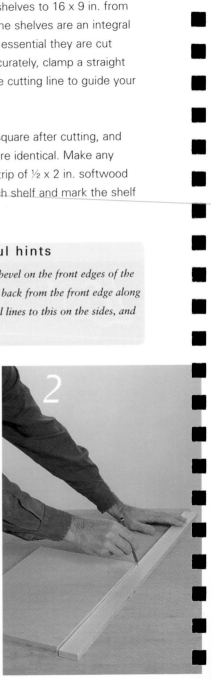

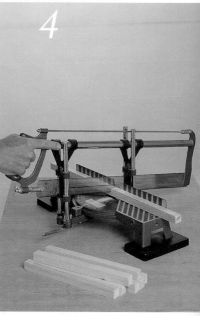

3   Set a miter saw to 90 degrees and cut the shelf fronts.
    If you have cut them accurately, they should be
    identical as well as fitting exactly to the shelves' long
    edges. Check that the shelf front ends are square and
    sand them smooth.

4   The eight shelf supports are 9 in. long, the same
    length as the shelf sides. Mark this measurement on a
    strip of 1 x 1 in. softwood. With the miter saw still set
    to 90 degrees, cut the shelf supports. Check that they
    are an accurate match to the shelf sides, then sand
    the ends smooth.

5 Each shelf support is glued and screwed to one side and a shelf, using two screws for each joint. To make sure the screws don't collide, butt the eight supports together using a square and mark a line 1½ in. from each end. Center the screw holes on these lines. Turn the supports onto the adjacent edge and mark lines and screw holes ¾ in. inside the first holes. Drill and countersink all the holes.

6 Cut the two sides to 54 x 12 in. from ¾ in. MDF. Butt the sides together at their back edges and mark a line for the back ¾ in. inside the back edges of the sides. Using a square and straightedge, mark the position of the shelf support bottom edges along both sides—the bottom ones 4 in. from the base, the middle two 14 in. above each top edge, and the top ones 10. in above the last top edge.

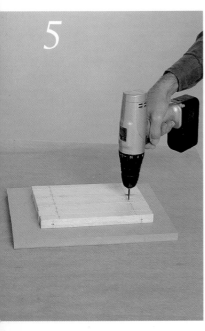

7 The shelf supports are screwed to the sides through the inner pair of pilot holes drilled in step 5. Position each support with one end butting up to the line for the back, use a bradawl to mark the screw positions in the sides, apply glue to the meeting edge, and drive in 1½-in. no. 6 screws.

8 Cut the back to 54 x 16 in. from ¾ in. MDF. Lay it flat and butt the sides up so the back fits in the drawn lines. Place the shelves in position on the supports, check the assembled carcass for squareness, then apply glue and screw the shelves onto the supports from below using 1½-in. no. 6 screws.

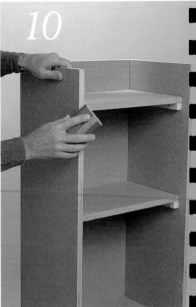

9 Check for squareness again and allow the carcass to dry completely. Mark the shelf positions on the back. Remove the carcass, lay it on its front and fit the back in place with the marked lines on the outside. Drill and countersink three pilot holes for each shelf with the outer ones 2 in. in from the edges, then insert and drive in 1½-in. no. 6 screws.

10 Stand the assembled bookcase upright and sand all the edges smooth with medium-grade abrasive paper wrapped around a cork or plastic sanding block. If you decide to sand a tiny bevel on the edges, make sure this is identical on each edge, otherwise the result will look sloppy.

11 Lay the bookcase on its back and apply glue to the front edges of the shelves—on this sort of length, regular dabs of glue are better than one thin, long line.

12 Place the shelf fronts in position and hold them there with masking tape, taking time to get the placing exactly right and pressing the tape firmly once you are satisfied. Allow to dry thoroughly, then apply primer to the softwood and paint in your chosen color.

Helpful hints

The shelf fronts are glued on because they are purely decorative and should not suffer rough treatment. If you prefer, you can reinforce the glue by hammering and center-punching small brads, then filling and sanding the holes.

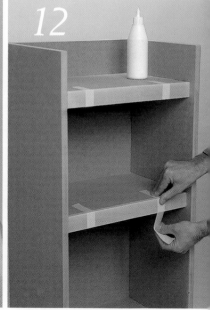

making a
window seat

The lid of this window seat fits into place and is also removable, giving you extra storage space as well as a place to read or look out the window. The seat here was made to fit a recess measuring 30⅜ in. long by 8⅝ in. deep—you can adapt the dimensions to suit the requirements of your own window space.

Materials (all lumber is softwood unless otherwise stated)

1 piece 25¼ x 1½ x 1½ in. • 2 pieces 7½ x 1½ x 1½ in. • 2 pieces 17½ x 1½ x 1½ in. • 2 pieces 3 x 1½ x 1½ in. • 2 pieces 35⅞ x 1½ x 1½ in. • 2 pieces 16⅜ x 1½ x 1½ in. • 2 pieces 4¼ x 1½ x 1½ in. • 1 piece 16 x ¾ x 1½ in. • 2 pieces MDF 18¾ x ¾ x 5⅝ in. • 1 piece MDF 37⅜ x ¾ x 18¾ in. • 1 piece MDF 37⅜ x ¾ x 15⅞ in.• 2½-in. no. 6 screws • 1½-in. no. 6 screws

Tools

Jigsaw • Crosscut saw • Backsaw • Sliding bevel • Carpenter's level • Combination square • Screwdriver • Drill with pilot and countersink bits • Straightedge • Pencil • Bradawl • Abrasive paper and cork or foam block • PVA (white) glue • Wood putty

Skill level
Advanced

Time
4–5 hours

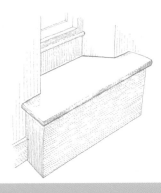

1 Measure up the back wall of the recess to the required
height—here, 18¾ in.—and use a carpenter's level to
mark a line along the back and the recess sides. Place
the body of a sliding bevel along the line at one of the
recess corners, set the blade to the angle, and lock in
this position.

2 Transfer the set angle from the sliding bevel to a piece
of 1½ x 1½ in. softwood, leaving enough at the end
for a saw cut, then cut the angle. Mark whether it is
the right or left side before repeating steps 1 and 2 at
the other corner of the recess.

3 Mark and drill three pilot holes in the back batten, then countersink them. Hold the batten in position and mark through onto the wall, then drill the wall and fit the appropriate wall anchors. Position the batten and drive in 2½-in. no. 6 screws.

4 Use the sliding bevel to fix the interior angles for the two recess side battens, then mark and cut pieces of of 1½ x 1½ in. softwood to fit. Hold each batten in place, overhanging the side wall, set the sliding bevel to mark the batten flush with the wall, then cut, drill, and fix to the recess walls.

5 Use the carpenter's level to mark a line the same height as in the recess along the side walls. Hold a piece of 1½ x 1½ in. softwood vertical to this line and mark the line, then make another mark on the wood 1½ in. below the first one. At the bottom, mark the height and depth of the baseboard onto the wood.

6 Clamp and cut the vertical batten to the shorter marked length, then reposition and reclamp it. Use a jigsaw or crosscut saw and backsaw to cut the recess for the baseboard. Place in position, check for fit, and adjust as required. When satisfied, mark the position with a carpenter's level and fix to the wall as in step 3. Repeat for the other side.

7 With both vertical wall battens in place, lay a long piece of 1½ x 1½ in. softwood across them, and mark the exact length of the top and bottom front frame members—here, 35⅞ in. Cut both pieces to length.

8 The depth of the seat carcass will partly depend upon the depth of your recess, and the length of the two floor plates will likewise be a variable factor. Here, 12 in. was suitable for the carcass, and we cut the two floor plates to 3 in. Place the floor plates in position, check that they are square to the wall, then drill, countersink, and screw in place.

Helpful hints

When screwing together two or more butted pieces of wood, remember to mark them out so the screws do not meet each other in the wood.

9 Lay the bottom frame member against the floor plates, place a piece of 1½ x 1½ in. softwood vertically on the end, and measure up to meet the line on the wall drawn in step 5, using a carpenter's level. Repeat on the other side, cut the vertical frame pieces to length, and drill and screw the four frame members together to make a rectangle.

10 Place the frame in position and measure from its inside edges to the wall; this should be the length of the floor plate plus the depth of the baseboard—here, 4¼ in. Cut two side horizontal pieces from 1½ x 1½ in. softwood, drill and screw them to the vertical wall battens, then drill and screw the frame in place against the vertical battens and the floor plates.

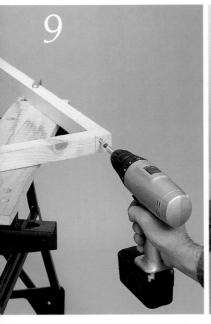

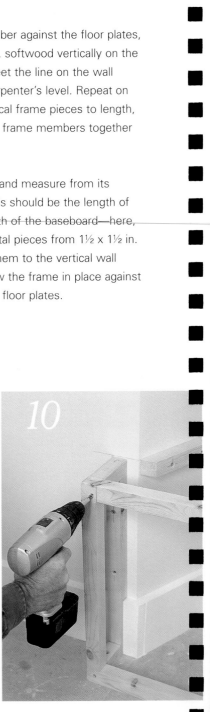

11 For the carcass sides, measure the outside of the side-frame assembly, including the recess for the baseboard, transfer to ¾ in. MDF, cut and fix to the sides as in step 5, this time using 1½-in. no. 6 screws. Repeat for the front, but including the depth of the MDF sides already in place.

12 For the dimensions of the lid, measure across the sides, adding ¾ in. on each side for the lid overhang, and the depth from the back of the recess to the front edge, again adding ¾ in. for the overhang. Transfer to a piece of MDF and cut to size. Place this against the walls on the carcass and use a square to draw lines from the recess/outer wall corners across the lid.

13 Measure the depth of the carcass along these lines and mark them at this point. Mark the recess inner corners across the lid with a square and straightedge, then mark the diagonal between the two sets of points. Shade in the waste, and cut the lid to shape.

14 Smooth the front and side edges of the top to a curve. You can use medium-grade abrasive paper wrapped around a sanding block, as here, or a power router and shaped bit. The end result should not cut into or scrape the legs of someone sitting on the seat.

Helpful hints

If you don't want a plain finish, consider adding some mitered molding as a rectangle on the front, or miter, fit, and paint baseboard to match the rest of the room.

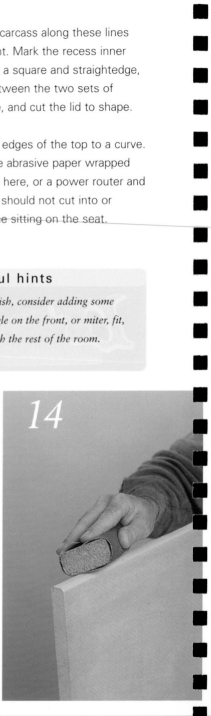

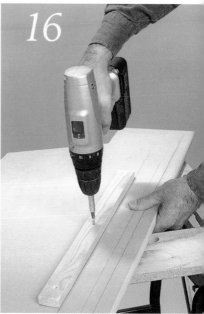

15 Place the top in position on the carcass and draw a line from beneath to mark the meeting point of the top and front. Make the line the full length of the front. Remove the top and lay it top-down, then draw a parallel line ¾ in. in from the front one to show the depth of the MDF, and a further line 1½ in. for the depth of the frame.

16 Measure and cut a lid batten from ¾ x 1½ in. softwood—the one here is 16 in. long. Mark, drill, and countersink pilot holes, lay the batten with its outer edge against the innermost of the three lines, mark through the holes, and drive 1½-in. no. 6 screws to hold it in place. Sand and paint the whole seat and lid to finish.

making an
accessory stand

With its crisp, modern lines, this accessory stand could be used anywhere in the house for storing magazines, bathroom accessories, fruits and vegetables in baskets, and so on. No joints are used in its construction—the skill comes in laying out and marking the pieces with accuracy, and in cutting miters with precision.

Materials (all lumber is softwood unless otherwise stated)

4 pieces 30¼ x 1¼ x 1¼ in. • 4 pieces 19 x ¾ x ¾ in. • 6 pieces 21¼ x ¾ x 2¾ in. • 6 pieces 20½ x ¾ x 2¾ in. • 10 pieces 19¾ x ¾ x ¾ in. • 1 piece MDF 19¾ x ¾ x 19 in. • 1½-in no. 6 screws • 1¼-in. no. 6 screws • 1-in. brads

Tools

Crosscut saw or jigsaw • Miter saw • Combination square • Straightedge • Bradawl • Pencil • Drill with pilot hole and countersink bits • Screwdriver • Abrasive paper and sanding block • Center punch • Hammer • PVA (white) glue • Wood putty

Skill level
Intermediate

Time
3–4 hours

1 Measure and cut the four legs to 30¼ in. from
1¼ x 1¼ in. softwood. Check that they are all identical,
then sand the ends smooth. Butt all four together
exactly and use a combination square to mark two
pairs of lines ¾ in. apart, with the first top line 11 in.
from the top edge of the legs, and the second top line
11 in. from the first bottom line.

2 Measure and cut the four slat supports to 19 in. from
¾ x ¾ in. softwood. Check that they are identical, sand
the ends smooth, then lay them out as in step 1. Mark
across the top edges for the positions of the five ¾-in.
slats—the outer ones starting 1¼ in. from the ends,
and the others with their centers at 5-in. intervals from
the outer ones.

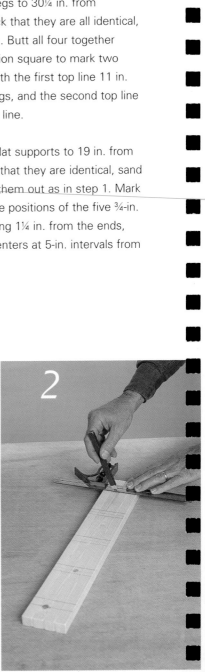

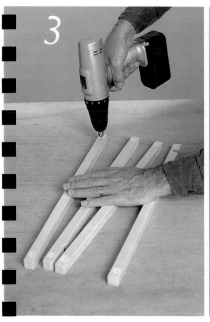

3 Lay the slat supports with the marked faces adjacent to the work surface. Draw lines 1¼ in. in from each end on the uppermost faces, then mark, drill, and countersink pilot holes through them.

4 Test-assemble one pair of legs with one pair of slat supports in position across the marked lines on the legs. Check for square, then apply glue to the meeting edges and drive in 1½-in. no. 6 screws. Repeat for the other pairs of legs and slat supports, clean off excess glue, and allow to dry.

5 Measure and cut the ten slats to 19¾ in. from
¾ x ¾ in. softwood, and check and sand as before.
Place the pairs of legs on their sides, clamp two scrap
pieces below the slat supports to hold them, apply
glue, position the slats on the supports' top edges,
and drive in 1¼-in. no. 6 screws through the outer
pilot holes.

6 Repeat for all the outer slats until you have
constructed a rectangular frame. Check for square,
then glue and position each of the other slats,
making sure the ends are exactly level, and drive in
the screws. Allow the glue to dry.

7 Set the miter saw to 45 degrees. Fit a length of ¾ x 2¾ in. softwood into the miter saw with about 2 in. over at one end. Cut the wood and smooth the cut end with abrasive paper.

8 Hold the wood to the marks on the legs with the mitered end protruding ¾ in. past one leg. Mark exactly where the other end meets a leg, then place the wood in the miter saw and cut, remembering the mark is the inside of the 45-degree angle. Mark this piece as a side or front/back rail.

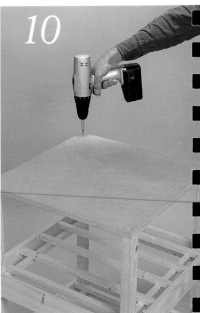

9 Continue to mark and cut the four lower rails—the sides should be 20½ in. and the front/backs to 21¼ in. Lay the frame on its side, position each rail, then mark and drive in 1-in. brads with a hammer. Make sure the brads are in line and equidistant for a neat finish.

10 Cut the top to 19¾ x 19 in. from ¾ in. MDF. Sand the sides smooth and check that they are square. Use a square and straightedge to mark lines 1¼ in. inside each edge. At the corners make diagonals inside the drawn squares, then drill and countersink pilot holes through the meeting point. Screw the top to the top of the legs using 1½-in. no. 6 screws.

11 Mark lines 1 in. from the top of the legs for the lower edge of the four top front/back and side rails. Cut and fit these rails to meet the lines drawn and the top edge as shown in steps 7 to 9.

12 Finish by using a center punch to drive all the nail holes below the wood surface. Fill these and the screw holes with wood putty and allow to dry. Sand the putty smooth, then apply wood primer and a top coat of your color choice.

Helpful hints

To ensure that brads don't split the wood surface, either use a tiny drill bit to make pilot holes beforehand, or snip the sharp ends off the brads and then hammer them in.

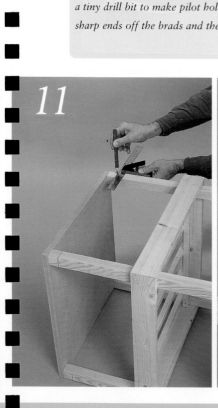

53

chapter 2
Shelving

fitting an **alcove shelf**

Fitting a shelf into an alcove is a popular way of making the most of space that would otherwise go to waste. The measurements given here are for a small-to-medium-size alcove, and you can obviously adapt them to suit your own requirements. The result is a sturdy piece of work that can take a surprising amount of weight—but don't push your luck by overloading it!

Materials (all lumber is softwood)

1 piece 45 x ¾ x 8 in. • 2 pieces 45 x 1 x 2 in. • 2 pieces 5¾ x 1 x 2 in. • 2½-in. no. 8 screws • Wall anchors

Tools

Backsaw • Crosscut saw • Sliding bevel • Carpenter's level • Square • Screwdriver • Drill with ¼ in., pilot, and countersink bits • Straightedge • Pencil • Bradawl • Abrasive paper and cork or foam block • PVA (white) glue • Wood putty

Skill level

Intermediate

Time

1–2 hours

1 Decide on the height of your shelf, then use a carpenter's level and pencil to mark the bottom edge of the shelf—that is, ¾ in. below where you want the shelf top to be—along the back wall. Extend this line across the whole wall, then match this line along the alcove sides to the length of your shelf minus 1¼ in.

2 To measure the exact length along the back wall, place the end of your measuring tape at one end and extend the tape. When you reach the other end, position the tape casing exactly in the corner and lock the tape. Make a mark at the visible end of the tape, take this dimension, and add the length of the tape casing, embossed along it.

3 Cut a strip of 1 x 2 in. softwood to length—here, 45 in. —then sand the ends square and with its top edge positioned along the line in the alcove, check that it is an exact fit. Drill pilot holes every 10–12 in. along this back support, and countersink the holes.

4 Hold the back support exactly in position on the back wall again, and use a bradawl to mark for the wall anchors through each screw hole. Make a cross for each, with the meeting point of the lines exactly over the bradawl marks.

Helpful hints

When measuring an alcove, never assume the length at the back wall is the same as at the alcove front. Always measure and check both lengths.

5 Fit a ¼-in. bit into the power drill, then drill through the wallboard at each X shape. Insert wallboard anchors, tapping them into place gently with a rubber mallet if necessary.

6 Place the back support into position on the wall, insert 2½-in no. 8 screws into each holes, and tighten them.

Helpful hints

You don't have to paint the shelf and its supports the same color—use any color combination you wish. Here, the supports were painted the same color as the wall.

7 Cut the side supports to the length of the line on the alcove sides—here, this is 5¾ in., the width of the shelf less 1¼ in. Drill and countersink two pilot holes in each support, then fix to the alcove sides as for steps 4–6. It is essential that the top edges of each of the supports are on an identical level.

8 Use a sliding bevel to check whether the front support will be the same length as the back one. Set the bevel to 90 degrees, and place it into each corner; a gap will tell you if there is a discrepancy. Set the bevel to the angle of one corner.

9 Transfer the bevel angle to the wood for the shelf, drawing it within the end of the piece to make cutting accurate. Mark the shelf back the length of the back support, then take the angle of the other corner and transfer it to the shelf at the mark, then cut. Sand smooth the ends.

10 Place the shelf in position on the supports and mark on the underside the front edges of the side supports. Remove the shelf and draw a line across the underside between the marks. Cut the front support to the exact length along this line.

11 Continue the line along the sides and top of the shelf, then drill and countersink three or four pilot holes for the front support. Place the front support in position, bradawl through the pilot holes, apply glue, and screw into place.

12 Reposition the front shelf on the supports. Mark, drill, and countersink pilot holes through the front support into the front edge of the side supports, then apply glue and screw into place. Fill all screw holes with wood putty, allow to dry, and sand smooth. Apply primer and a top coat of paint.

Helpful hints

To make less work for yourself, you can buy ready-made wooden shelves from most hardware stores. These usually have shaped or molded front edges.

making a
hall shelf

This simple hall shelf uses a basic dado joint to hold the back in place. These joints are all about accurate marking and cutting—the ideal situation is where you are only using glue and screws to reinforce a good, tight, fit. To gain confidence using a power jigsaw, draw patterns and profiles on sheets of waste lumber, MDF, or plywood, and practice your control and accuracy on them.

Materials (all lumber is softwood)

1 piece 32 x 1 x 7 in. • 2 pieces 12 x 1 x 5½ in. • 1 piece 30 x 1 x 7 in. • 1½-in. no. 6 screws • 1½ in.-brads • 2 brass coat hangers and screws

Tools

Crosscut saw • Backsaw • Straightedge • Combination square • Jigsaw • Screwdriver • Drill with pilot hole and countersink bits • Hammer • Abrasive paper and cork or foam block • PVA (white) glue • Wood putty

Skill level

Beginner

Time

1–2 hours

1 Measure and cut the pieces to size from 1 in. soft-wood. The two uprights are 12 x 5½ in., the top is 32 x 7 in., and the back 30 x 7 in. Check that the corners are square on all pieces, and sand the ends smooth with abrasive paper wrapped around a sanding block.

2 Place the two uprights exactly together along their sides. Pin them together and drive in brads to hold them. Transfer the profile to one of the sides, and shade in the waste wood to be cut out.

Helpful hints

You can get inspiration for profiles on the uprights by looking at old furniture, or from books on folk-art patterns and profiles. Remember, however, the aim of the game is strength.

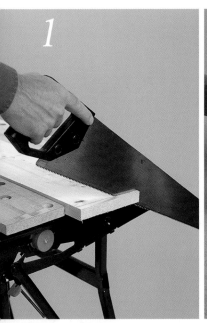

3 Clamp the uprights on a bench or work surface, and use a jigsaw to cut out the profile. Position the jigsaw guide just on the waste side of the pattern line, and move the jigsaw smoothly. With the uprights still clamped, use the abrasive paper and block to get a smooth, identical shape.

4 Remove the uprights from the clamp. To draw the dado joint, lay flat one upright and place the end of the back piece against one side corner. Carefully draw around the edge of the back.

5 Repeat step 4 for the other upright, making sure you position the back on the appropriate corner. Shade in the waste wood, then clamp as before and cut out the dado joints with a crosscut saw or jigsaw.

6 Measure ½ in. along the sides and front from the corners on the top. Draw a diagonal between the end marks and cut the miters off, then sand down the rough edges using abrasive paper wrapped around the cork block.

Helpful hints

To fit the shelf to a wall, before painting, drill and counter-sink two screw holes in the back, Hold the shelf to the wall, check that it is level, and mark the screw holes. Drill the wall, insert wall anchors, and screw the shelf in place.

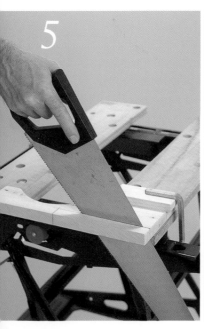

7 Fit the back panel into place in the dado joints in the uprights. Make any adjustments for a close fit, check for square, then hold in place and drill and countersink three equidistant pilot holes through the back into the uprights. Apply glue to the meeting edges, and insert and tighten 1½-in. no. 6 screws.

8 Place the top in position, and drill and countersink two equidistant pilot holes into the uprights. Drill two more holes into the back panel, then disassemble, apply glue, and insert and tighten the screws. Fill all the screw and brad holes with wood putty, and sand smooth when dry before painting.

making a
shelf with coat rail

The principle behind this project is the same as for the hall shelf on page 64; the difference is that for this one you need to make up wall plates to hold a metal coat rail. The dimensions here are for an alcove 45½ in. wide and 20 in. deep; you can adapt the cutting sizes to suit your own requirements.

Materials (all lumber is MDF unless otherwise stated)
2 pieces 14 x ¾ x 6 in. • 1 piece softwood 44 x 1 x 3 in. • 1 piece 45½ x ¾ x 7½ in. • Coat rail 44 in. x ¾ in. diameter plus ends and screws • 1½-in. no. 6 screws • Wall anchors

Tools
Crosscut saw or jigsaw • Combination square • Sliding bevel • Straightedge • Bradawl • Pencil • Drill with pilot hole and countersink bits • Screwdriver • Abrasive paper and sanding block • Carpenter's level • PVA (white) glue • Wood putty

Skill level
Intermediate

Time
2 hours

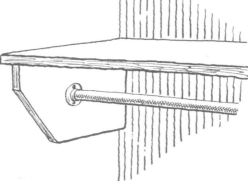

Easy home improvements

1 Mark a line for the top of the wall plates and batten along the side and back walls of the alcove, using a carpenter's level on each wall. Make sure this is accurate, otherwise the shelf will not sit correctly.

2 Cut the two wall plates to 14 x 6 in. from ¾ in. MDF. To match the width of the batten, draw a line 3 in. from the top edge across the length of each plate. Set the combination square to 45 degrees and mark an angle to the bottom edge from this line. Shade the waste.

Helpful hints

Always check the angle of the alcove side walls to the back one; it may look like a perfect right angle, but assuming that it is without checking can ruin a project.

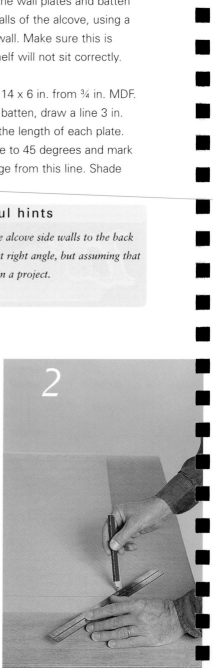

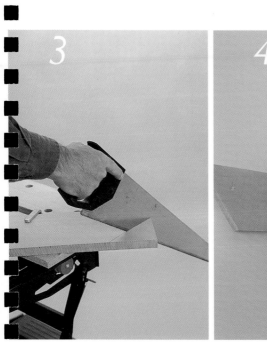

3 Clamp one wall batten to the workbench and use a crosscut saw or jigsaw to cut off the waste MDF. Smooth the cut edges with abrasive paper wrapped around a block, then repeat for the other wall plate.

4 Drill and countersink two pilot holes about 3 in. from the ends along the line. Hold the wall plate in position, mark the wall through the holes, then remove the plate, drill the wall, and insert wall anchors. Position the plate again and screw into place. Repeat on the other side wall.

Measure between the wall plates at the back—here, the length was 44 in. Cut a piece of 1 x 3 in. softwood to length and sand smooth the ends. Drill and counter-sink three pilot holes at equidistant intervals, then hold the batten in position and mark the wall holes. Drill and fit anchors in the wall as before and screw the batten in place.

Mark on the wall plates for the rail ends, remembering to allow for lifting coat hangers above the rail. Measure between the wall plates for the length of the rail; stretch the tape measure across, and when the tape and the casing fit perfectly, lock the tape and add the length of the casing to that shown on the tape.

7 Transfer the measurement to the metal rail—here, the
45½ in. alcove, less the two ¾-in. wall plates, gave a
length of 44 in. Clamp the rail securely and cut it
accurately with a hacksaw. Smooth off the cut edges
and hold in position with the ends in place, bradawl
the screw holes in the plates and drive in the screws.

8 Measure across the back wall of the alcove for the
back of the shelf. Hold the sliding bevel to get the
angle of the side wall, lock the bevel and transfer the
angle to ¾ x 7½ in. MDF. Repeat on the other wall,
then cut the shelf. Sand smooth the ends, position on
the batten and wall plates, drill and countersink pilot
holes, then glue and screw the shelf in place.

chapter 3
Closets

making a
shoe rack

On floors or in closets, shoes and boots have a way of expanding to fill the space available, so this rack should provide a tidy answer to that problem. The construction is quite straightforward, but the real skill lies in the measuring and marking out—take your time and be prepared to check everything more than just once.

Materials (all lumber is MDF unless otherwise stated)

2 pieces 32 x ¾ x 13 in. • 1 piece 32 x ¾ x 20 in. • 1 piece 20 x ¾ x 3 in. • 12 pieces softwood 20 x 1 x 1 in. • 1½-in. no. 6 screws • 1¾ -in. brads

Tools

Jigsaw or crosscut saw • Miter saw • Combination square • Screwdriver • Drill with pilot and countersink bits • Straightedge • Pencil • Bradawl • Hammer • Abrasive paper and sanding block • PVA (white) glue • Wood putty

Skill level

Intermediate

Time

2–3 hours

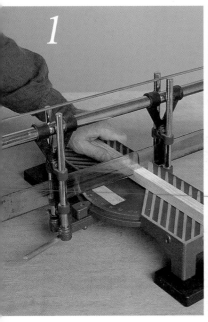 

1 Set the miter saw to 90 degrees and mark and cut twelve pieces of 1 x 1 in. softwood to 20 in. This is where a miter saw is particularly useful, because the sawn ends will be all but square.

2 Even with the miter saw, you must check the ends for square. Lay flat a few pieces at a time, and butt them up to a flat surface, then use the combination square to check that they are identical in length and are square. Sand the ends. For the back, mark and cut a piece of ¾-in. MDF to 32 x 20 in.

3. Mark and cut the MDF for the front kick to 20 x 3 in. Cut the two MDF sides to 32 x 13 in., then mark out the top miters—join a line starting 4 in. from the back edge and 4 in. down the front. Shade in the waste, cut both miters, and check that they are identical before sanding all the MDF pieces smooth.

4. Lay the sides down with their back edges together and their top and bottom edges meeting exactly. Mark a line ¾ in. inside from the meeting edge lengthwise along both pieces. From these lines, mark across the sides for the positions of the back rails: the bottom one 2 in. from the bottom, then the middle one 10 in. above that, and the top one 10 in. farther.

5 The lines across the sides represent the top edges of the back rails. Stand a rail on end with its top edge meeting the line and its back edge against the lengthwise line, then mark around the rail. Draw diagonals between the corners for the pilot hole center, then repeat for all the rails on both sides.

6 From the lengthwise lines, measure 8 in. along the horizontal lines and mark at this point. Use a square to measure up 4 in., and mark this for the top point of each front rail.

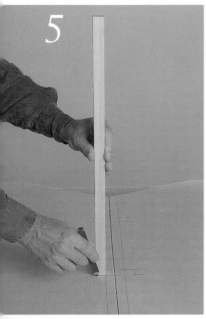

7 Draw a line from the top back edge of each top rail to the top points of each front rail. Position each front rail along this angle with the top point meeting the mark, then draw around each rail as in step 5.

8 Fit a small bit in a power drill, and drill pilot holes at each diagonal center, working from the inside out. Clean off the waste on this side. Turn the sides over, then fit a countersink bit into the power drill and countersink the holes from the outside.

Helpful hints

Drilling pilot and guide holes is often thought of as a minor part of a project, but badly centered ones can mar the look of a piece as well as lessening the strength. Hold the drill square to the workpiece and apply pressure smoothly.

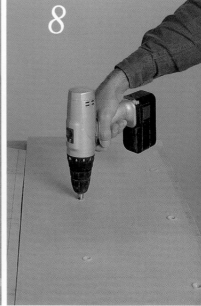

9 Lay down the back and sides, with their inside edges butted up exactly to the back. Using a square and straightedge, mark lines across the back between the bottom back rail lines on the sides. This must be an exact fit, or the rack will not fit well.

10 Apply glue to the back rails, position them on the lines across the back, then nail 1½-in. brads every 4–6 in. along the rails. Clean up any excess glue before it dries completely.

Helpful hints

You can keep shoe-cleaning materials, spare shoelaces, shoe trees, and so on in the space behind the front kick and beneath the bottom rails.

11 Hold each side up square to the back with the side back edges flush to its rear edge, then mark, drill, and countersink pilot holes every 8–10 in. Apply glue, insert 1½-in. no. 6 screws, and tighten.

12 Use a bradawl through the back rail pilot holes, then apply glue, insert the screws and tighten them. Hold each front rail in position, then repeat this process. Place the front kick in position, then mark for pilot holes and fit as in step 11. When the glue is dry, sand the whole piece and paint it.

making a **wardrobe with loose cover**

If you don't have alcove space in your home, or don't want to purchase or make solid closets or wardrobes, free-standing clothes racks are a great way to hang your clothes. Living with them uncovered, however, can be rather like living in a department store. Designed to take in a single rack, this wardrobe incorporates a simple, easily assembled frame and a six-piece denim cover.

Materials (all lumber is softwood unless otherwise stated)

4 pieces 60 x 1¼ x 1¼ in. • 4 pieces 28⅜ x 1¼ x 1¼ in. • 4 pieces 19⅜ x 1¼ x 1¼ in. • 8 pieces plywood 7¾ x ⅛ x 6¼ in. • 4 pieces plywood 6 x ⅛ x 5 in. • 1-in. no. 6 screws • 1 piece chambray denim 62 x 32½ in. • 1 piece chambray denim 32½ x 23¼ in. • 2 pieces chambray denim 62 x 23¼ in. • 2 pieces chambray denim 62 x 19 in. • 2 pieces chambray denim 36 x 3 in.

Tools

Crosscut saw or jigsaw • Combination square • Straightedge • Bradawl • Pencil • Drill with pilot hole and countersink bits •

Screwdriver • Abrasive paper and sanding block • Scissors • Pins • Needles • Basting and sewing threads • Tailors' chalk • Yardstick • Sewing machine

Skill level

Intermediate

Time

4–5 hours

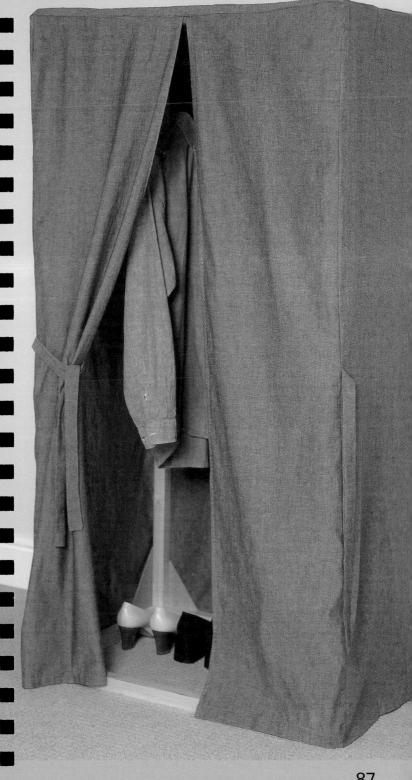

1 Cut the four frame uprights to 60 in., the four front and back rails to 28⅜ in., and the four side rails to 19⅜ in., all from 1¼ x 1¼ in. softwood. Check that each set of four pieces is identical in length, and sand the ends. Lay two upright and two side rails together to make a rectangle, check for square, then drill and countersink pilot screw holes. Drive in 1-in. no. 6 screws.

2 Repeat for the other upright and side pieces. Mark, drill and countersink pilot holes for the front and back rails in both rectangular assemblies, making sure the holes do not crash into the screws already in place. Hold each rail in position, check with a square, then push a bradawl through the pilot hole before driving in the screw. Repeat for all the rails until you have a square-corner frame.

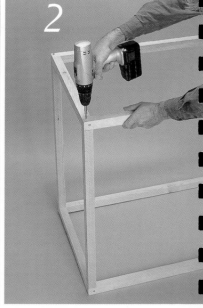

3 Mark out four 9-in. squares and two 7¼-in. squares on a sheet of ⅛ in. plywood, then mark one diagonal across each square. Clamp to the workbench and cut out the squares with a fine-tooth crosscut saw. Saw across the diagonals on each square to make two triangles.

4 Use a square to mark cutting lines from the square edges of the triangles—the eight triangles for the sides should be 7¾ x 6¼ in., and the four for the back 6 x 5 in. Cut to size, then hold each one in turn in position, just inside the edges of the frame, then drill and countersink pilot holes and screw in place.

5 All the pieces of fabric can be cut from a single 48-in.-wide piece 7 yd. long. Lay out the fabric and use tailors' chalk to mark the back to 62 x 32½ in., the top to 32½ x 23¼ in., the two sides to 62 x 23¼ in., the two front pieces to 62 x 19 in., and the two ties to 36 x 3 in.

6 Cut out all the pieces with scissors, making sure you cut accurately to the chalk lines. It's a good idea to pin the pairs of pieces together with a paper label so you don't get confused later.

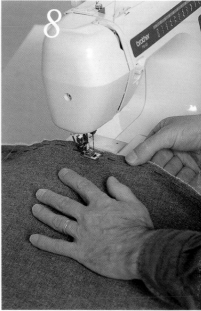

7 Pin one long edge of each side piece of denim to the corresponding length of the back, and pin the top to the back in the same way. Baste the joins using contrasting-color thread.

8 Sew the joins together using matching-color thread on a sewing machine. The seam allowance for all the joins should be ½ in. Turn the joined pieces inside out to check that your seam is straight—this is the procedure for all seams throughout this project.

Helpful hints

As well as pinning two pieces of fabric along the edges that will be basted and sewn, insert a few pins elsewhere in the body of the fabric to ensure that it does not slide or move out of position.

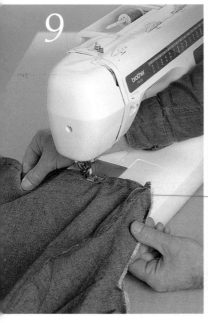
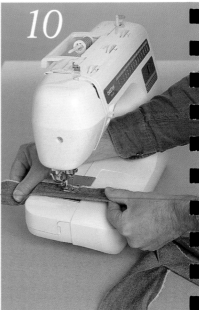

9 Turn the front edge of the top back ¼ in. and sew this flat using a zigzag stitch. Repeat for the long front edges of the side pieces. Pin the sides to the top, baste as before, then stitch in place.

10 Fold one long tie in half along its length. Sew across one end then along the length, leaving the other end open. Turn the tie inside out and press it flat, then hand-stitch the opening. Repeat for the other tie.

Helpful hints

It's vital that you fit brand-new needles in your sewing machine before starting a new project, especially when using a heavy fabric like chambray denim. Check that they're the right size, too.

11 Position one front piece against one side and place the middle of one tie across the seam line on the outside. Pin and baste this front seam to join the front, side, and tie, then sew the three pieces together. Repeat for the other side.

12 Tuck the top edges of the front under, then pin and baste them before sewing with a zigzag stitch to a neat, flat finish. Place the cover over the frame, then pin up the hem all around at the bottom. Remove the cover, press the hem flat, and stitch it.

fitting an
alcove storage unit

If storage space is tight, being able to use all the space in your home becomes a priority. Alcoves so often are just filled with clutter, but some thought and imagination can transform them into efficient and attractive storage modules. The dimensions here are for an alcove 45 in. wide and over 20 in. deep. A word of warning about the chest of drawers: don't use a valuable heirloom or something you think may be one day!

Materials (all lumber is MDF unless otherwise stated)
1 piece 45 x ¾ x 17 in. • 1 piece 72 x ¾ x 17 in. • 2 pieces 17 x ¾ x 15¾ in. • 1 piece 16 x ¾ x 6 in. • 5 pieces softwood 16 x ¾ x 1 in. • Hanging rail 25 x ¾ in. diameter • 1½-in. no. 6 screws • Chest of drawers 31½ x 18 x 18¼ in. • Wall anchors

Tools
Crosscut saw or jigsaw • Miter saw • Hacksaw • Combination square • Straightedge • Pencil • Carpenter's level • Drill with pilot hole and countersink bits • Screwdriver • Abrasive paper and sanding block • Bradawl • Adhesive tape

Skill level
Intermediate

Time
4–5 hours

1 Place the chest of drawers against one side wall of the alcove and check that it is square with a carpenter's level; you may have to add wedges to straighten it. Cut one piece of ¾ x 17 in. MDF to the required height—here, 72 in.—and stand it square against the chest side. Check with the level, then mark the height and draw a line along the back wall.

2 Remove the upright and use the carpenter's level to mark a line along the alcove side walls. To find the front edges of the top piece, mark a line vertically from the front of the chest along the side wall, and join this to the horizontal line.

3 Measure the distance for the top batten along the chest-side wall—this should be about 1 in. less than the depth of the top. Mark and cut a piece of ¾ x 1 in. softwood, and bevel the underside of the front edge with a miter saw set to 45 degrees. Next, drill and countersink pilot holes, and screw to the wall using wall anchors.

4 Measure across the alcove and cut the top to size— here, 45 x 17 in. from ¾ in. MDF. Replace the upright against the chest and check for square, then lay the top in place, resting across the upright and on the batten. Check with the carpenter's level, then mark a line for the bottom edge on the other side wall.

5 Remove the top and upright. Measure and cut the wall plate from ¾ in. MDF, again 1 in. or so short of the top and wide enough to take the hanging rail—here, 16 x 6 in. Drill, countersink, and fix to the wall as for the batten on the opposite side.

6 Measure and cut four more battens, adding a bevel to the front edge as before. Drill, countersink, and fix two to the wall as in step 3, replace the upright and use a carpenter's level to mark across to the upright.

Helpful hints

If your chest of drawers is not very heavy, remove the bottom drawer, drill through the back, and fix this to the baseboard behind with screws.

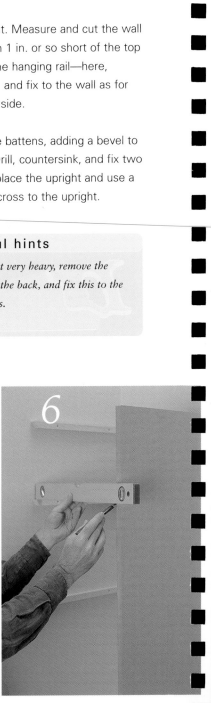

7 Stand the upright against the back wall and draw lines for the inner battens along the upright, using a square and straightedge. Drill, countersink, and fix the battens to the upright using 1½-in. no. 6 screws.

8 Place the upright in position against the chest again, check for square, and get an assistant to hold it exactly in position while you drill through the upright into the chest side, countersink, and insert and tighten screws. For stability, it's best to screw at the top and bottom of the chest.

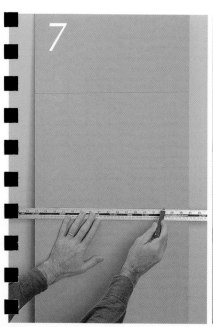

9 Replace the top, then measure and mark the batten, wall plate, and upright edges from below. Remove the top and use the lines to mark, drill, and countersink pilot holes. Replace the top in position, then insert and tighten screws.

10 Measure across between the wall and the upright for the shelves, then cut to size from ¾ in. MDF—here, they were 15¾ in. long and the same width as the upright. Place each in turn on its battens, and plane or sand as necessary for a close fit. The shelves in this project are free-standing and removable. If you want to fix them to the battens, do this before screwing on the top, and work from the bottom one upward.

11 Measure the length for the hanging rail across the tall unit, and cut the rail with a hacksaw. Tape the fittings on the rail ends, hold the rail up to the desired height, and mark the screw holes on the wall plate. Mark on the upright, using a carpenter's level to ensure straightness.

12 Bradawl the screw holes in the wall plate and upright, then use the screws supplied with the hanging rail hardware to fix it in place. Remove the rail and fixings before sanding and painting the unit, then replace when the paint is completely dry.

Helpful hints

The height of the shelves above the chest of drawers will depend entirely on what you want to use them to store. If in doubt, make them equal distances between the chest top and the unit top.

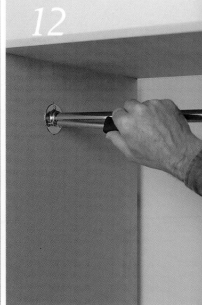

fitting louver doors

Ready-made louver doors are available in set heights and widths from many hardware and lumber stores. They are a good way to either create an attractive closet front for an alcove, as shown in this project, or you can use them to replace plain-front old closet doors anywhere in the house. Make sure you fit them with the louvers facing down.

Materials (all lumber is softwood)
2 pieces 84 x 2 x 2 in. • 1 piece 42½ x 1 x 2 in. • 1 piece 6 x ¾ x 2 in. • 1 piece 84 x 1 x 4 in. • 1 piece 24 x 1 x 4 in. • 1 piece 45 x 1 x 8 in. • 1½-in. no. 6 screws • 2½-in. no. 6 screws • 2 louver doors • 6 brass 2-in. flush hinges • 2 wood handles • 2 magnetic door catches

Tools
Crosscut saw or jigsaw • Combination square • Straightedge • Bradawl • Pencil • Drill with pilot hole and countersink bits • Screwdriver • Abrasive paper and sanding block

Skill level
Intermediate

Time
3–4 hours

1 Measure out from the back wall of the alcove or closet along both side walls. If you already have shelving or units in place (see pages 56 and 94), allow a little room in front of them; otherwise, make sure you have enough space for the wall battens to be fitted comfortably into the alcove.

2 Use a spirit level to mark a line for the outer edge of the wall batten on one alcove wall, then extend the line to the full height of the batten. Because not every alcove has right-angle corners, use a square from this first line to draw across the front of the alcove, thus ensuring that the battens will be square to each other. Mark for the other batten.

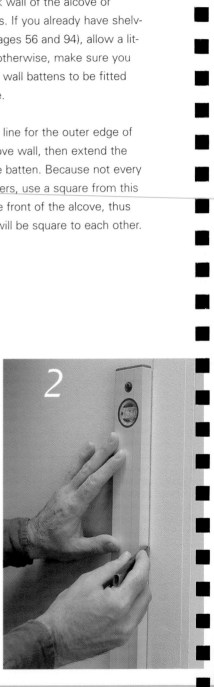

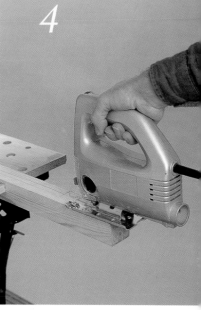

3 Cut the wall battens to length from 2 x 2 in. lumber—
here, 84 in.—then stand one upright to its marked line
on the wall (an assistant can do this), checking it with
a spirit level. Use a square to mark the height and
depth of the baseboard on the batten, then mark any
curved profiles. You can mark the baseboard shape
onto a paper template.

4 If you used a template, transfer the profile onto the
bottom of the batten. Clamp the batten to the workbench and use a jigsaw to cut the profile. Remove the
batten and check it against the baseboard, making
adjustments to the profile until it fits snugly in place.
Repeat steps 3 and 4 for the other batten.

5 Drill and countersink pilot holes through each batten, hold it in place, and mark through the holes onto the wall. Drill and insert wall anchors, then screw the battens in place using 2½-in. no. 6 screws.

6 Measure and cut the floor plate to fit between the baseboards of the alcove walls from 1 x 2 in. wood—here, it was 42½ in. Drill and countersink pilot holes to fit to the front of the battens, making sure they don't meet any holes through the battens into the wall. Screw into place using 1½-in. no. 6 screws.

Helpful hints

If you don't have an assistant to hold the doors for you, use wedges to keep them at the right height when measuring and fitting.

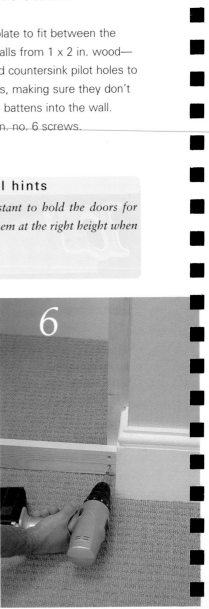

7 Cut the back wall plate to 6 in. from ¾ x 2 in. wood, and drill and countersink pilot holes. Mark the back wall with a line the same height as the battens, then center the plate and fix as for the battens. Cut the front upright to the same length as the wall battens from 1 x 4 in. wood, and the horizontal front-to-back piece, to fit to the alcove back wall, from the same lumber. Screw them together, checking at each stage for squareness.

8 Center the front upright and horizontal piece across the floor plate and resting on the wall plate, check with a spirit level, then drill and countersink pilot holes through the front and into the wall plate from above. Drive in 1½-in. no. 6 screws.

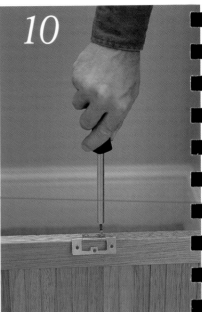

9 With an assistant holding each door in place and allowing a small gap at the bottom for opening and closing, make a mark ⅛ in. above the top on each wall batten. Cut the frame top piece to the width of the alcove—here, 45 in.—from 1 x 8 in. wood. Fit this to the marks, mark, drill, and countersink pilot holes, then screw into place.

10 For doors of the height used here, you will need three 2-in. brass flush hinges per side—shorter doors can use two. Allow a minimum distance of 4 in. from the top and bottom for the outside hinges, and position the third one equidistant between the others. Make pilot holes with a bradawl and screw the hinges in place.

11 Get an assistant to hold a door in place to a wall batten, with enough allowance so the door can open and close smoothly. Position the hinges against the batten and bradawl pilot holes for the hinge screws. Drive in the screws firmly, checking that the door functions properly. Repeat for the other door.

12 Mark the positions of the magnetic catches on the frame upright and inside faces of the doors with a bradawl. Screw on the catches, making sure they allow the doors to lie flat against the upright. Fit the handles to the doors.

Helpful hints

For a lasting finish on the doors, use one or more coats of clear, matte varnish. After filling and sanding the screw holes, paint the frame to match the wall color.

glossary

Batten – a narrow strip of wood; often used to describe such a strip used as a support for other pieces

Bevel – any angle other than a right angle at which two surfaces meet

Butt joint – a simple joint where two pieces of wood meet with no interlocking parts cut in them

Countersink – to cut, usually drill, a hole that allows the head of a screw, nail, or brad to lie below the surface

Crossbar – molded wood separating glass panes

Dado – a shallow, wide groove cut across the grain of a piece of wood; a dado joint is one where a piece of wood is fitted into a dado

Galvanized – screw or nails covered with a protective layer of zinc; used mainly for exterior work

MDF – medium-density fiberboard; a prefabricated material that can be worked like wood

Miter – a joint made by cutting equal angles, usually at 45 degrees to form a right angle in two pieces of wood; cutting such a joint

Pilot hole – a small-diameter hole drilled into wood to act as a guide for a screw thread

Rabbet – a stepped, usually rectangular, recess cut along the edge of a piece of wood as part of a joint

Rail – a horizontal piece of framing in a door or window

Ripping – sawing wood along the grain

Softwood – wood cut from trees like pine, maple, and cedar, belonging to the botanical group *Gymnospermae*

Stile – a vertical piece of framing in a door or window

Template – a cut-out pattern on paper or cardboard, used to help shape wood

Upright – a vertical piece of wood used in making a frame or carcass

index

acknowledgments

All photographs taken by Alistair Hughes, except for:

8/9 Camera Press; 54/55 Lucinda Symons/ Robert Harding
Syndication; 76/77 Rowland Roques-O'Neil/ Robert Harding
Syndication

Illustrations by Stewart Walton.